HOUGH END HALL
THE STORY

Andrew Simpson
& Peter Topping

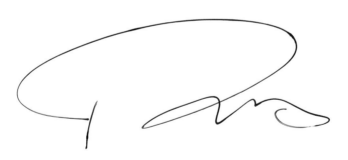

TOPPER PUBLISHING

About the Authors

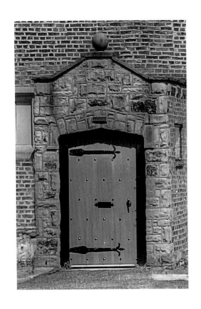

Peter Topping and Andrew Simpson have been working together for a number of years developing projects linked to the history of south Manchester. It is, as Peter said, a collaboration where he paints the pictures and Andrew tells the stories. Their work has appeared in venues across South Manchester, including an 80 metre mural, which was commissioned by a large building company and opened by Lord Bradley of Withington in 2012. Both also work independently.

Peter's work is much admired and he regularly exhibits his work, showcasing it on his website at www.paintingsfrompictures.co.uk/paintings

Andrew recently published a book on the history of Chorlton-cum-Hardy in 2012, writes articles on local history and produces a popular history blog at www.chorltonhistory.blogspot.co.uk and is currently working on a new book on Manchester and the Great War.

First published 2015.

Topper Publishing
39 Lambton Road, Chorlton-cum Hardy,
Manchester, M21 0ZJ.

ISBN 978 1 943093 40 3

Typesetting and origination by Topper Publishing
Printed in Great Britain.

Contents

Acknowledgements

Carolyn Kagan whose idea it was to "Make Hough End Hall Ours".

Peter Topping who steered the project along the roller coaster campaign.

The Friends of Hough End Hall Committee who have worked tirelessly to achieve our aims.

Manchester City Council for letting us use the old images in their archives.

Michael Thompson - Hardy Productions for photographs and videos.

Oliver Bailey whose family farmed and later bought Hough End Hall and who supplied many of the details for the building and surrounding farmland in the 1950s and 1960s.

Marjorie Homes who always knew something that no one else did.

Philip Lloyd who supplied some fine photographs of The Hall in the late 19th century.

Roger Shelley who took some iconic pictures of The Hall in the 1960s and whose work can be viewed at https://www.flickr.com/photos/photoroger/

Paul Thompson who owned The Hall and ran it as a restaurant providing a fascinating glimpse into The Hall's later history.

Faith Waldren whose memories of playing in the hayricks and riding the bumps in the 1950s gave us a different view of Hough End Hall.

All the people, groups and organisations that supported our project.

Nora Templar who lived at nearby Dog House Farm and whose father drew the picture of Alexandra Park Aerodrome in 1924.

Dave Wilcox for his photograph of the staircase.

Introduction

Hough End Hall has one of those long and rich histories which pretty much has all you would want from a building dating back to 1596.

It was built by Sir Nicholas Mosley who made his fortune in London and was gambled away by one of his descendants a century and bit later.

Its first owner had been at the heart of national politics during the reign of the first Elizabeth, another of the Mosleys saw The Hall and estates temporally confiscated by Parliament during the Civil War, after which the place settled down and fell out of the great events of State finally ending up as humble farm house for two centuries.

Since then it has faced a number of challenges, from those who wanted to demolish it, to those who radically knocked it about in the name of commercial enterprise and those who walked off with some of its prize features and should have known better.

To the casual visitor, the interior today has nothing of that rich history and even the outside, has according to some experts been amateurishly restored.

But that is to miss The Hall's place in the history of our community. Having once been the centre of a large estate and then a farm of over 200 acres it became in the 20th century a place of which many will have fond memories.

And now it enters one of its most exciting phases in its long history as a group of local people seek to buy it and transform it into an asset for all.

In the space of just a year and a bit the campaign to "Make Hough End Hall Ours" has raised local awareness of the importance of the building, including its rich history and just what it could offer the community.

PART ONE
A jewel of a building home to the Mosley family from 1596 until the mid 18th century

Blakeley chap:

Newton

Claton hall

MANCHESTER

Ashton Vnder lyne

Garret hall

Garton chap:

Denton

Denton hall

Du

Hughhall

Redysh

verton chap:
Diddesbury
ton: O

Goythal

H

Mac

STOPFOR

A fine new house, a present from a grateful monarch, picking the wrong side in the Civil War and the loss of the estate by "reckless extravagance".

Sir Nicholas Mosley built The Hall in 1596 and his new house befitted a man who, at the age of nearly fifty had left Manchester for London where he prospered and was rewarded by Queen Elizabeth 1 for his service to London and his country with a knighthood and *"a handsomely-carved oak bedstead, together with some other articles of furniture, for the new house which he had recently erected at Hough End, on the site of the old mansion which his ancestors had inhabited."* [1]

Now the Mosleys had been at Hough End from at least 1465 but there are no descriptions of the earlier family home although The Hall does appear on Saxton's map of 1577.

It would have been a substantial timber house which by the 1590s I guess would no longer have been fit for purpose, particularly for a man who walked with royalty and had just purchased the manor of Withington.

So our new hall was built to reflect all that was new and fashionable.

1 Mosley, Sir Oswald, Family Memoirs, 1849, Printed for Private Circulation, page 6

It was a traditional Elizabethan brick house designed to imitate the letter E.

On the ground floor there was the hall which took up most of the building with the long gallery directly above it.

These long galleries were a feature of Elizabethan houses and were used for a variety of purposes from displaying the family portraits to a place to walk when the weather was poor.

The kitchen and living areas were contained in the two arms that jutted out from the main part of the building.

Like most homes of the period it would have had a garden which included a variety of plants from flowers to herbs used in cooking and medicines.

The wide range of herbal treatments included things like anemone which as a juice was applied externally to clean ulcerations and infections, burdock which when crushed and mixed with salt could be used on dog bites, flatulence and tooth pain and wood betony good for headaches, belching, cramps, convulsions, bruises and even killing worms.[2]

Along with these was mugwort for

Sir Nich. Mosly — Clothworker.
Lord Mayor of the City of London 1599.
Engraved from an Unique Print in the Collection of
Sir John S.t Aubyn Bar.t

Published as the Act directs Sep.t 1.1798. by W.Richardson, Castle Street, Leicester Square.

2 Culpeper, Nicholas 1616-1654, The English Physician, 1652. Culpeper was a botanist, herbalist, physician and astrologer whose two books The English Physician and the Completer Herbalist are a collection of pharmaceutical and herbal knowledge. The English Physician has been almost continuously in print since the mid 17th century. He was a radical during the English Civil War translating medical and herbal texts into English from Latin as self help guides for the use of the poor.

inducing labour and assisting birth, after birth and easing labour pains.

It is of course impossible now to accurately recreate what the Mosley family would have seen from the windows of their new home.

To the north and east was Chorlton Brook which in parts

Old St Clements Circa 1512

would have flowed through woodland some of which was still in evidence in the 19th century.

To the west across open land was the road from Didsbury into Manchester and just a little further west beyond that was the village of Chorlton with its chapel, while a mile away was the equally impressive Barlow Hall, home of the Barlow's.

All of which must have made it a pleasant retreat for Sir Nicholas from both the bustle of London and Manchester.

According to the Mosley family biography written in 1849 *"after having served the office of high sheriff for his native county of Lancaster in 1604, he passed the remainder of his days at his favourite mansion, where he expired at the age of eighty-five, and was buried in the church of Didsbury in which a handsome mural monument was erected to his memory by his second wife"* in 1612.[3]

3 Ibid Mosley, Sir Oswald, page 9

Now I have no way of knowing exactly what he would have been doing in his fine house but his will suggests he was active in the community bequeathing *"five poundes ev'ie yeare during twentie years next after my decease oute of rentes of the Denorie of Bridge North, yearlie to bee receaved"* for the *"scoole att Chollerton Chapelle."* [4]

That same will offers up a little insight into how The Hall was furnished, for on his death Sir Nicholas bequeathed *"to my said wife in lieu of her chamber two of my beste beddes wth the ffurniture accordinglie, excepte the beste tapestrie cov'ringe and the beste bedstocke alsoe excepted.*

Also I give and bequeath unto my said wife all such plate as she had att the tyme I married her, save onlie one pot wch was stoolene away in the tyme of my mayroltie in London .... And alsoe I give and bequeath unto my saide wife my coache and coaches horses wth the furniture thereof; and alsoe all such Lyyens as were my said wife before I married her, and a resting in the house." [5]

4 Booker, Rev John, A history of the ancient Chapels of Didsbury and Chorlton, 1857, Chetham Society page 132
5 Ibid, Booker, page 132

In turn when Elizabeth Mosley died she passed her velvet curtains, two of her beds with the *"valences, crimson cov'ringe and the furniture thereunto belonginge, my better greate boxe with a drawing tyll therein, one needleworke cushion twoe crimson ymbroydered cushions, ...three gardes of velvet, the one halfe of all such lynnens"* to her servant Elizabeth Tatton and a bed, linen and cushions to her other servant Margaret Hartley.[6]

The inventory of *"her goods and possessions"* made on May 24 1617 also recorded that she left *"Three tuns, one great salte with a cover, a trencher salt, a standing salt, three boules, twoe dozen spoones, twoe cannes, one broken boule and broken silver – all waying 174 oz,"* along with napkins and table clothes.[7]

All of which is not the most comprehensive insight into the contents of Hough End Hall but it will have to suffice.

During the Civil War the family's support for the King led to a degree of financial difficulty and letters written from The Hall in the late 1640s chart the problems, but with the Restoration in 1660 the Mosleys like many Royalists, saw their fortunes restored.

Sadly for Hough End Hall there isn't a happy ending. The dissolute and extravagant life style of the last family member in the words of the Mosley biographer *"reduced his splendid patrimony and he sold without remorse the whole estate."* [8]

6 Ibid, Booker page 143

7 Ibid, Booker, page 146

8 Ibid Mosley, page 31

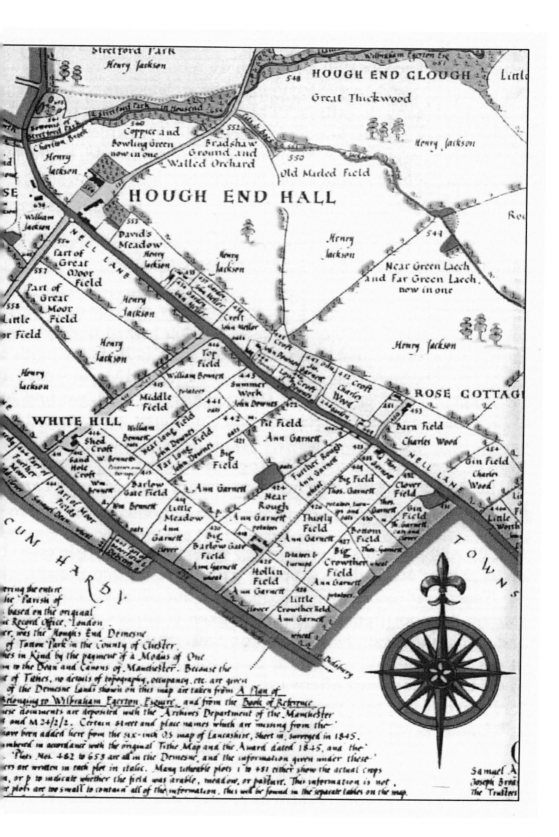

Stretford Park
Henry Jackson

HOUGH END GLOUGH   548   Littl

Great Thickwood

Coppice and
Bowling Green
now in one
Henry
Jackson
Bradshaw
Ground and
Walled Orchard   550   Henry Jackson

Old Marled Field

HOUGH END HALL

David's
Meadow
Henry
Jackson   Henry
Jackson   Henry
Jackson   544

Part of
Great
Moor
Field   Henry
Jackson   Near Green Laech
and Far Green Laech
now in one

Part of
Great
Moor
Field   Croft John Mellor   oats

Little
Field   Henry
Jackson   Croft
John Mellor
oats   Henry Jackson

William Brwen   Top
Field   potatoes   Summer
Work
John Downes   oats   Croft
Charles
Wood   ROSE COTTAG

Middle
Field   John Downes   Pit Field
Ann Garnett   Barn Field   Charles Wood   454

WHITE HILL   William
Brwen   oats   Near long Field
John Downes   Further Rough
Ann Garnett   Big Field
Thos. Garnett   Clover
Field   Gin Field
Charles
Wood

Shed
Croft   W. Brwen   Far long Field
John Downes   Ann Garnett   potatoes turn   Thos.
Garnett   Little
Worth

Sand
Hole
Croft   Wm.
Brwen   Barlow
Gate Field   Ann Garnett   Near
Rough
Ann Garnett
potatoes   Thistly
Field   Bottom
Field   Gin
Field

Wm Brwen   Little
Meadow
Ann
Garnett   Barlow Gate
Field
Ann Garnett   Ann Garnett   Thos. Garnett   Big
Crowther
Field
Ann Garnett

Big
Field
clover   potatoes &
turnips   Thos. Garnett

Hollin
Field
Ann Garnett

Ann Garnett   Little
Crowther field
Ann Garnett   potatoes

CUM HAR DI)

ering the entire
he Parish of
based on the original
Record Office, London
r, was the Hough's End Demesne
of Tatton Park in the County of Chester.
hes in Kind by the payment of a Modus of One
to the Dean and Canons of Manchester. Because the
of Tithes, no details of topography, occupancy, etc. are given
of the Demesne Lands shown on this map are taken from A Plan of
belonging to Wilbraham Egerton Esquire, and from the Book of Reference
ese documents are deposited with the Archives Department of the Manchester
and M24/2/2. Certain street and place names which are missing from the
ave been added here from the six-inch OS map of Lancashire, Sheet 11, surveyed in 1845.
umbered in accordance with the original Tithe Map and the Award dated 1845, and the
Plots Nos. 482 to 653 are all in the Demesne, and the information given under these
ers are written in each plot in italic. Many tillable plots 1 to 451 either show the actual crops
a, or p to indicate whether the field was arable, meadow, or pasture. This information is not
r plots are too small to contain all of the information, this will be found in the separate tables on the map.

TOWNS

Samuel A
Joseph Bra
the Trufters

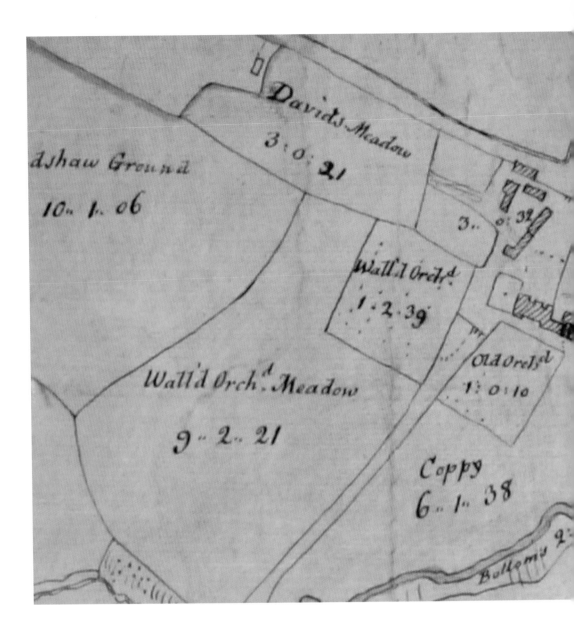

And with that The Hall passed into the possession of the Egertons who rented it out to a succession of tenant farmers.

But that change of owner has provided us with one of the most exciting maps associated with The Hall.

Above is the land map of the area from the mid 18th century, and for me it is priceless because it offers up the chance to walk the fields of south Manchester in 1768.

Here recorded are the names of the fields, some of the owners and some of the buildings close by The Hall.

And what is remarkable is that a full 78 years after our map was made virtually all the fields marked still had the same names.

It is just a little example of historical continuity but one that allows us to move from the last years of the Mosley occupancy into that new one when tenant farmers worked the fields and were mindful of the boundaries with their neighbours.

But that is not all, for our map of 1768 yields up one curiosity which is that it appears the wrong way round and so what should be north is shown at the bottom of the map, but when reversed and transposed onto modern maps it is a perfect match.

Nor is that all because given its date, it may be the earliest representation of The Hall in any real detail and shows that the "walled orchard" along with the "old orchard" were there by the mid 18th century and raises a fascinating line of enquiry into the Bowling Green and the small water course that fed off from Chorlton Brook presumably to supply the house along with whatever wells may have been dug.

It may also have fed the huge pond opposite Sandy Lane which can be seen in many of the photographs from the early 20th century.

Such is the power of this map to fix The Hall at the centre of the history of its location.

PART TWO

Two centuries at the centre of a farming community from the mid 18th century to 1940

A farmhouse, the Lomas family and a way of life unchanged for two centuries.

It is easy forget that The Hall's days as the home of well to do and powerful people accounted for only half its existence. For over 200 years from the 1750s into the middle of the last century it was a farmhouse and where once the Mosley family deliberated on matters of trade and high politics, in their place there were families of tenant farmers.

Some of these we know by name like Henry Jackson and the Lomas family but most are at present lost to us.

They rented the land from the Egerton estate and during most of the 19th century farmed over 200 acres stretching east into Withington and west up to the borders of Chorlton-cum-Hardy.

This was one of the largest farms in the area with Henry Jackson in 1841 employing ten labourers who lived in The Hall and possibly more who lived in their own homes nearby and the size of the farm is further vouchsafed by a list of the contents which were put up for auction in 1849.[9]

9 Manchester Guardian, January 20 1849

Amongst the list for sale were "*about 300 thraves of wheat, 600 thraves of oats, 80 thraves of horse beans, 100 tons of hay, 100 loads of potatoes of various sorts, 30 tons of Swede"* [10]

All of which were typical of the style of farms in the area and compare with the contents advertised just six years later at Red Gates Farm which is now the site of Chorlton Library and the much smaller farm of the Bailey family on Beech Road in Chorlton.

Henry Jackson remains a shadowy figure. We know that a Henry Jackson was baptised at the chapel in Chorlton in the February of 1771 and his parents were Samuel and Sarah Jackson of Withington who may have occupied The Hall.

But this would have put him a full ten years older than his age on the 1841 census.

All that we do know is that his death in 1847 opened the way to the Lomas family who took over the tenancy and were still there in 1940.

By then the farm had shrunk to little more than the immediate land around The Hall and with the death of Sarah

Hough End Hall. *Chorlton-cum-Hardy.*

10 A thrave equates to two dozen, and was the number grouped together as a bundle when stacked in the fields.

Lomas in the September of 1940 the tenancy of what was left was taken over by the Bailey family of Park Brow Farm and run alongside their existing farming business.

And it is from them along with some written accounts dating from the 1880s and a survey carried out by the Egertons in 1938 that we have a very good idea of how the once elegant Elizabethan hall was transformed into a work a day farm house.[11]

11 In 1938 the Egertons produced a survey of The Hall and surrounding buildings which is currently lodged in the Archives and Local History Library at Central Reference Library in Manchester in the Egerton Papers M24. The Survey is complemented by the memories of Oliver Bailey whose family rented and later bought The Hall

Mrs Williamson in 1888 wrote that "*the mansion itself has been little altered outwardly since its erection by Sir Nicolas Mosley, excepting that the large entrance porch, which was formerly at the end now occupied by the tool house, is removed and several antique windows have been replaced by modern ones.*

Internally everything is changed; in fact, the only trace of former grandeur is the ornamentation of the tool house. A handsome carved oak staircase, which until quite recently led from the tool house to an upper chamber, has been taken by Lord Egerton to Tatton, and there certainly shows to more advantage." [12]

12 Williamson, Mrs C, Sketches of Fallowfield, John Heywood, 1888, Page 48

It was now she concluded "*a comfortable substantial farm house.*"

A little earlier in 1862 an unknown visitor recorded that "*the walls of several rooms are wainscotted at the top, one in particular has a border around the edge of the ceiling with a reed of bead moulding. The panels are square, 15 inches across and quite plain, except those over the fireplaces which are ornamented with inlaid geometrical devices. Some of the choicest wainscotting has been removed, it is said, to adorn a Cheshire house belonging to the Egertons.*" [13]

On the ground floor the central part of the building along with the north wing had become small rooms including a dining room, sitting room, kitchen and bathroom to the left of the entrance and a drawing room to the right.

Most remarkable of all was the conversion of the south wing into a smithy which remained in use well into the 1950s.

The first floor consisted mainly of bedrooms, some belonging to the family and others at the rear for the labourers who Henry Jackson and Samuel Lomas employed.

13 A Visit to Hough End Hall in Withington, Ashton Reporter December 6, 1862, quoted by Renshaw, Cliff, FRICS, Hough End Hall 400 Years of History, 2001 page 33

The practice of accommodating some of the workforce within the family home was common across the north and had mutual benefits. For the farmer it pretty much guaranteed a workforce for the duration of the annual contract and for the labourer ensured board and food.

Of course the wages paid to the labourers were lower compared to those who lived out but their board included a bed, food and in many cases the simple domestic chores of having clothes mended and washed.

The system particularly suited young men and women leaving home for the first time. Of the ten living with Henry Jackson in 1841 six were 15 or younger, another three were 20 and only Michael Rustage was in his mid 30s.

So for the families of Henry Bent aged 12, Margaret Cain aged 15 and Helen Platt and Sophie Owen aged 20 there must have been a degree of reassurance that their children were secure in a place they knew.

More so because for some of the 19th century it was still the custom to settle up a labourer's wages at the end of the year, deducting any advances made.[14]

The Lomas family continued to employ and board agricultural labourers throughout the 19th century and as late as 1915 Mrs Lomas was advertising for *"A Youth for milk round; live in."*[15]

Sadly no pictures of the interior of The Hall during this period have come to light and by the time the young Oliver Bailey was exploring the property, the furniture belonging to the Lomas family had long gone.

But not quite everything, for upstairs in the mangle room was *"an old mangle that was basically a large box full of cobbles that rolled back and forth on rollers on the wooden base when it was worked by turning the handle."* [16]

It will have been used by Mrs Lomas and may well have been more than half a century old by the time Oliver saw it.

Somewhere there may still be some of their furniture along with some of their family papers and photographs, but at present all that has turned up is a postcard sent to the family sometime between 1910-1915 and a photograph of the young Lomas children in the garden of The Hall.

These were John born in 1888, Ethel Mary in 1891, Constance Amy in 1899, and Eveline in 1910.

None of our three look to be much older than twelve and possibly younger which would place them in the garden sometime at the beginning of the last century.

By then The Hall which had been a farmhouse for two centuries still had another sixty years of busy activity, but even

14 For a detailed description of pay and working conditions in Chorlton-cum-Hardy and Withington in the mid 19th century see, Simpson, Andrew, The Story of Chorlton-cum-Hardy, the History Press 2012

15 Manchester Evening News February 1915

16 Oliver Bailey, June 2014

before then its future was far from certain.

As more of the surrounding land was developed for housing and a new road was planned to run past The Hall, its very existence was threatened.

But that grim grey future is for another time, instead I shall close with a description of The Hall in 1857 shortly after Samuel Lomas had taken up his tenancy when it was still an impressive sight, leading one observer to write that its " *ivy-covered walls, its clustered chimneys and its gabled roof, present a picturesque and pleasing appearance.* " [17]

17 Ibid, Booker, page 167

PART THREE
An uncertain future... the 20th Century

A plan to demolish it, save it as a Coronation event and its long lingering decline as a building.

Even before Mrs Lomas died in 1940 The Hall was threatened by demolition, lingering neglect and more than a touch of vandalism.

It began with the removal of that fine oak staircase sometime just before 1888 by the Egertons by which The Hall had *"few points of interest, having been a good deal modernized"* [18]

But that was nothing as compared to the plan to build a new road through The Hall in the spring of 1921 which would have also meant the destruction of a fine avenue of trees.

The subsequent outcry and campaign organised by Mr John Swarbrick led to the establishment of 'A Hough End Preservation Committee' which proposed an alternative route.[19]

18 A History of the County of Lancaster: Volume 4, William Farrer & J. Brownbill, editors, 1911
19 Hough End: A scheme for saving The Hall, Manchester Guardian March 24, 1921

The Corporation amended their plans and The Hall was saved but its fate remained a major preoccupation both of the Preservation Committee and the Ancient Monuments' Society which was established in 1924.

The society appointed a special committee in 1932 to explore possible uses for The Hall of which three appeared to have some chance of success. These were *"an advanced Art Gallery or Museum for Manchester," "A Hall of Residence for the Manchester University"* and *"a home for a number of learned societies, including the Ancient Monuments' Society itself."* [20]

The Hall was found to be in a remarkably good state of preservation and *"the owner Lord Egerton, expressed a willingness to give the hall if a suitable use could be found for it. He stipulated however that the farmer's widow should have right of tenancy for the rest of her life and this restricted the use of the building for an indefinite period"* [21]

20 Ancient Monuments Society's Transactions, Ancient Monuments' Society, 1975 page 57

21 Ancient Monuments Society's Transactions page 57

The Art Galleries Committee of Manchester Corporation were at first enthusiastic about converting it into a branch gallery and Sir Oswald Mosley offered to give family pictures and furniture associated with The Hall if it became a museum. These included the carved oak bedstead presented by Queen Elizabeth 1, a long carved sideboard marked "N.M" and a

portrait of Sir Nicholas copied from the original in Chetham's
Hospital along with a print inscribed "Sir Nicholas Mosley
Clothworker, Lord Mayor of the City of London 1599"

Sadly the Corporation decided that the cost of supervising
"art treasures in a multiplicity of small rooms such as those at
Hough End Hall," was prohibitive.

And while its future as a Hall of Residence seemed to have promise this too came to nought when the Government cut the grants it awarded to Universities for capital projects during the Depression.

There were other innovative plans for a future use ranging from a folk museum put forward by the Historical Association in 1930 to renewed calls for the Corporation to take it over.

These culminated in a petition calling for *"the picturesque Elizabethan manor house, and the land around to be secured for the city by the corporation and suitably preserved and laid out as an ornamental flower garden in the Elizabethan manner."* [22]

It was argued that this would be a fitting Coronation memorial marking the accession of King George VI, but like all

22 Preservation of Hough End Hall, Manchester Guardian December 19, 1936

the earlier plans it came to nothing.

Undaunted by this set back Mr Swarbrick continued to argue for The Hall's preservation.

In 1937, the Guardian published his suggested layout of the ground facing the southern front of The Hall including a grand fountain, spacious lawns and bordered by ornamental bushes.

Just what Mrs Lomas *"the farmer's widow"* thought about the continued attempts to give her home a new purpose is unclear.

She continued to live in the property till her death in 1940 by which time with the war in full swing considerations of preservation took a back seat.

The Hall and the remaining three acres were taken over by the Bailey family who farmed Park Brow Farm.

They used some of the outbuildings for their own pigs and chickens and rented out the remaining ones.

"In 1958 following the death of the last Lord Egerton we took the opportunity to buy both the hall and the land although the field to the rear of the Hall was the subject of a compulsory

purchase order by Manchester Council who planned to build a school on the site." [23]

But this new phase was to be a short one for within four years The Hall was sold to a developer and the last link with two centuries of farming came to an end.

23 ibid Oliver Bailey

PART FOUR
When the developer came knocking, 1962-2010

The sale of The Hall, a succession of developers that "botched" restoration and new ventures.

The uncertain future which had pretty much stalked The Hall from the early decades of the last century continued into the 1960s.

Its days as the home of the rich and powerful were long

gone and without its farm it no longer had a purpose as a farmhouse.

   Added to this it was now in need of repair and was suffering from being empty and at the mercy of vandalism.

   The Corporation continued to show no interest in buying The Hall and the Bailey family who had bought it *"were fighting a losing battle against the enormous costs of maintaining a large, infirm mansion."* [24]

And so once again its future was in doubt. Sadly there was no wealthy benefactor or organization willing to buy; restore and use the property which just left a developer who was prepared to *"restore the empty building for residential use and to build an office block near to it."* [25]

Some amenity groups supported the plan but the Corporation objected on the grounds that the area was zoned for residential use and that *"the building of the new block to preserve the old hall was too high a price and that the offices with between 300 and 500 workers would harm the amenities of the district."* [26]

So began a torturous few years where fresh plans were submitted and rejected and new ones put down on the table. The Corporation continued to object to some details in the development plans while insisting that any deal must come with a promise to restore the building.

24 Waterhouse, Robert, Hall, or nothing at all, the Guardian April 21 1973

25 Tudor Manor Saved Appeal Upheld, Guardian September 29, 1962

26 ibid Guardian, September 29, 1962

Along the way the proposed petrol station part of one submission was dropped and the developers undertook that "*restoration should 'retain the original character.' All external materials must be 'similar to or in keeping with those originally used' and that there were to be no additions or alterations."* [27]

The agreement was finally signed in December 1965 and the first of the two office blocks which obscure The Hall today was built.

This was Crown House with 25,000 square feet of office space spread over four storeys and built just to the south of The Hall, with its car park resting on what had been the garden of the house.

27 ibid Waterhouse

41

Mauldeth House followed in 1973 and dwarfed both its neighbour and The Hall rising seven storeys and offering 50,000 square feet of space.

The restoration of The Hall was met with some consternation leading to the comment by the secretary of the Ancient Monuments Society that the work had been *"botched and included reconstituted stone for the window mullions, sills and heads, and that the inside had been gutted."* [28]

Today it is impossible to work out what of the interior had been lost in that restoration and what was to vanish later.

28 Bulmer-Thomas, Ivor, letter to the Manchester Evening News, January 1969

The present false ceilings hide imitation oak beams which in turn obscure what might be original timbers.

This will no doubt be a disappointment to the many who dined in The Hall under what they thought were the very timbers put in by Sir Nicholas back in 1596.

But it points to the fairly frequent changes of use that made for a heap of alterations.

Not that this should be much of a surprise, for despite its purchase by developers there was no clear idea what it should become. One night club owner showed an interest and there was *"talk of a restrained dinning out place with Cromwellian decor."* [29]

During the late 1970s and 80s it did become a successful restaurant and continued as such until 1991 when it was sold and converted into offices, a phase which was short lived and after another brief spell as a restaurant The Hall became vacant, looking for both a new owner and a new purpose.

29 ibid Waterhouse

PART FIVE
Looking for ghosts and staircases...
memories of The Hall from the 1950s

A ghost, a pond, plenty of old buildings and many memories.

The one thing that is pretty much missing from the history of The Hall are the memories of the people who lived, worked and played there.

In its entire 400 years or so there are but a scant few and most of these are contained in the living memory of people who knew the place during the last half century and a bit.

Some are those fragmentary recollections based on adventures on warm summer evenings trespassing in the grounds and peering in through the unwashed windows into The Hall itself.

Others centre on daring but dangerous forays into the outhouses ever mindful of being caught but driven on by the promise of forbidden excitement and the chance to scrump a few apples.

Most have been long forgotten and are only coming out of the shadows as this part of The Hall's history gains wider attention.

So for some The Hall was the "haunted house" and for others it was a place to go looking for the tunnels which according to popular belief led to Barlow Hall and somewhere close to the present bus terminus on Barlow Moor Road.

My friend Faith recalled adventurous days playing by the Bumps which was that stretch of land running east alongside the Brook behind The Hall and sitting beside the hayricks on those hot days in late summer with all the pervading smell of the hay.

June remembered, *"that we used to hang about here nearly every night"* while Veronica remembered the geese and the mysterious window.

Some memories are accompanied by a photograph and one

in particular that has always fascinated me is of three girls sitting on the low wall which ran along Nell Lane looking across at the geese, with Hough End Hall away to our left and the farm buildings containing the pig sty belonging to Mr Bailey and Jimmy Ryan's rabbits on our right.

I don't have a date but the young girl in the middle with the striped jumper is Miss Veronica Jones which I guess places the picture sometime in the early 1940s.

She told Peter that they were there on the wall *"feeding geese and then 'snuck' up to look in at the window as a dare."*

Others too recalled exploring The Hall, working their way through the silent rooms constantly expecting to be caught but driven on by a wish to find treasure and evidence of that ghost.

Needles to say the searches proved fruitless but there were always the old outhouses which acted as a magnet for both the young of the area and for Roger Shelley who in the mid 1960s took a series of photographs which captured a bunch of lads doing what all such lads will do when presented with empty buildings.

What is all the more remarkable is that some at least are known to us and a few still live in the area over 45 years after they posed for these pictures.

Nor are they the only local people with more recent memories of The Hall.

There are plenty who have come forward with stories of the nights when they ate under the imitation Tudor beams when The Hall was a restaurant and of a whole range of social gatherings from parties to weddings and even funerals.

Paul Thompson who owned The Hall from 1979 till 1985 recalled that *"funerals played an important part of their business along of course with Christmas parties which during one December generated 6,000 covers."* [30]

But of all the recollections it is those of Oliver Bailey which do most to unlock the story of The Hall in the late 1940s and 1950s.

30 Thompson Paul, August 2014

His family had taken on the tenancy in 1940 and continued to rent the land and buildings until they bought them in 1960.

The memories provide a rich insight into what the interior of The Hall was like along with descriptions of the outbuildings, fields and some of the daily routines which will not have been so different from those undertaken by Henry Jackson and Samuel Lomas.

They begin with the pond which features in some at least of the old pictures and was a place Oliver and his brothers played as no doubt had the Lomas children before them.

In his case it was to use the model steam boats they had made in their spare time and which they would take down to water's edge and test with more than a hint of competitive spirit.

I like that image which will strike a chord with anyone who grew up in 1950s when a lot of how you occupied your spare time was self made.

Unlike Oliver I never experimented with homemade fireworks but like him and many of my friends those long summer holidays included wandering off for the day with just a sandwich, a drink and a vague notion of when you would come home.

These in themselves are delightful evocations of a lost time but there is much more about The Hall, the layout of the farm buildings and the surrounding land which help us understand the last phase of Hough End as a working farm.

They begin with the interior of The Hall which was still as it had been when it was a farmhouse.

Mrs Lomas the last resident had died in 1940 and while her furniture had gone, the rooms remained a testament to what the place had been like for over two hundred years and echo exactly the plan of the building made in 1938.

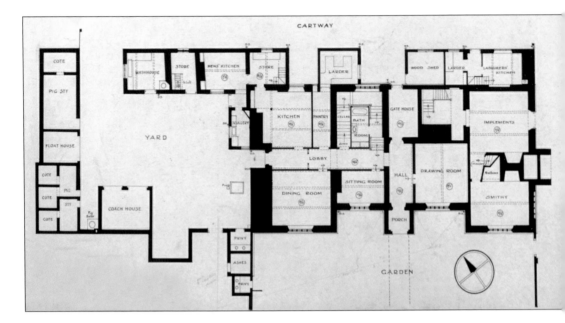

On the ground floor the central part of the building along with the north wing were small rooms including the kitchen and bathroom to the left of the entrance and a drawing room to the right.

The smithy which took up the ground floor of the south wing was still in use, and Oliver told me that *"I remember a man called John Hallsworth had his blacksmith shop there in the 1950s.*

He had been a blacksmith with British Road Services and rented the smithy at Hough End from my father after he retired from BRS and there was a wooden staircase up the wall of the hall inside the smithy itself.

He was into wrought iron – he made a couple of gates for Park Brow Farm.

However, Sam & Jack Priday - who were farriers with a smithy in Withington - came round and used the forge to shoe my father's Suffolk Punch horse." [31]

31 ibid Oliver Bailey

The first floor consisted mainly of bedrooms, along with the mangle room which was above and just to the right of the main entrance which still had *"an old mangle that was basically a large box full of cobbles that rolled back and forth on rollers on the wooden base when it was worked by turning the handle."* [32]

At the time it was still possible to access the second floor which by then was empty but may once have been bedrooms.

But equally fascinating are the descriptions of the out houses and the farm yard all of which show up on the 1938 plan commissioned by the Egertons and include pig sties, copes, the coach house, a wash house and the pig boiler. [33]

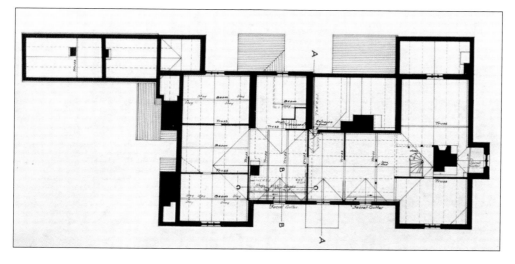

32 ibid Oliver Bailey
33 Egerton Papers M24

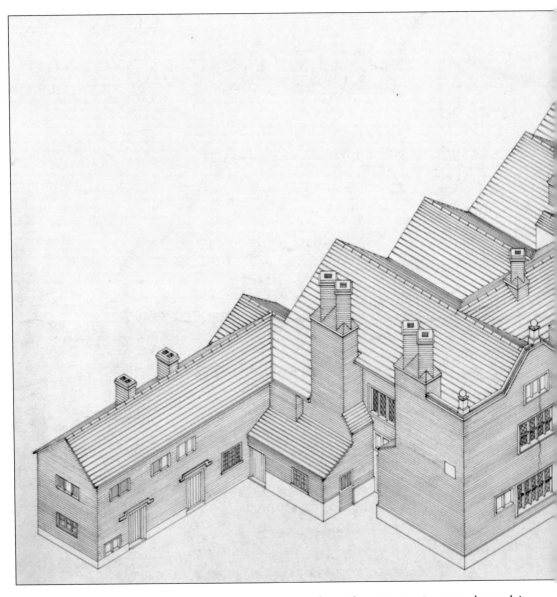

These were all cleared away after the property was bought by the developers and so Oliver's account is all we have to supplement that plan.

"To the right of the hall there were various add-on outbuildings at the back, probably nineteenth century.

One was a cottage and another had been a storehouse of some sort that had fallen into disrepair.

Along the side of the plot that borders Mauldeth Road there was a field and in front of that a line of what had been loose boxes where my father kept pigs and the ones nearest Nell Lane were used for horses for a while.

As kids we kept ours there, Silver, Nils and Betty when they weren't out in the fields.

Later on there was a pair of Russian Wolfhounds Michael and Heather and after they went, two Irish Wolfhounds Terry and Fergus that later moved to Park Brow Farm

At the far end of the same building, nearer the Hall in one of the lofts a man called Jimmy Ryan bred rabbits for show as a hobby.

He worked at MetroVick as a day job and later joined Boeing in the US.

On the corner of Nell Lane and Mauldeth Road there was an L-shaped building and on the lower level my father kept pigs and on the upper level he had about 200 deep litter hens.

When there were no pigs it created a severe problem of frost as the pipes kept freezing up in winter and one of my jobs was to use a blowlamp to thaw them out and fix the occasional burst so the hens could drink.

It was in that same yard we finally captured the St Kilda ram that had led us and the police a merry dance from the field near Chorlton Station, along Wilbraham Road and St Werburgh's Road.

We cornered it in a pen we put together from the show jumps from Didsbury Show that were stored there.

At one time my father had Highland cattle in the field where the school now stands and also kept them in the field near Chorlton.

He also had a peacock with a couple of peahens and for a period Hough End was nicknamed Peacock Farm because of the noise they made and because the peacock used to fly across Nell Lane into the park so lots of people saw it.

There was a deep depression in the field near the rear left hand corner of the plot of the Hall itself and it was made by a bomb dropped there during the second world war, certainly it was known as bomb crater corner. According to family history the blast knocked my father over – he was an ARP Warden during the war so could have been out at night on fire watch.

During the war there was a riding school at Hough End where my sisters learnt to ride horses. The horses were kept in the loose boxes in the long building parallel to Mauldeth Road." [34]

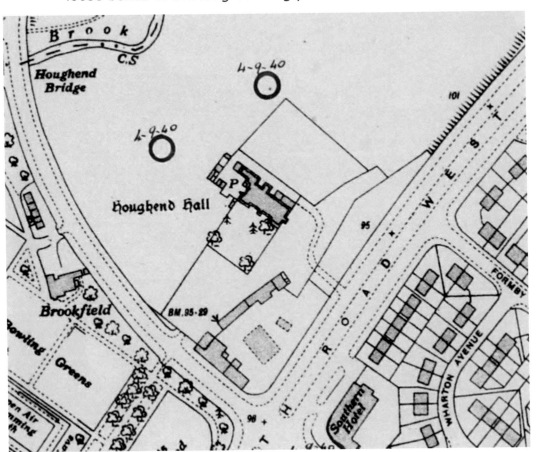

34 ibid Oliver Bailey

It is one of those things about memories that they do constantly reveal aspects of the story that were never recorded or have been forgotten. There may be a reference to the riding school in a directory of the period and we might just strike lucky with more recollections of the place.

In the meantime I want to return to that picture of Miss Veronica Jones and her friends sitting on the wall which Oliver remembers ran the length of the west side of The Hall and was *"about four feet high and topped with flags to give a flat top maybe 18" wide. These had been tied together with iron straps set in sockets in the flags that had been filled with molten lead but most had rusted away in my time."* [35]

It is one of those tiny bits of The Hall now long gone which connects us not only with Oliver and Miss Jones but takes us back past Mrs Lomas and the other tenant farmers perhaps even to the days of the Mosleys which is a fitting point to close.

35 ibid Oliver Bailey

PART SIX
"We fear the true country aspect of the place is at an end." Mrs Williamson 1888

A fine 18th century house, creeping urbanization and an aerodrome.

Hough End Hall did not of course exist in isolation. During its years as the home of the Mosley family it was only one of a number of fine country homes.

Just a mile away was Barlow Hall and away to the east was the old medieval manor house of Withington.

And from sometime around 1750 if not earlier there was Brook Croft House which almost faced The Hall and is still there today. The house is now known as Brookfield House.

Once it stood in its own grounds surrounded by fields with the brook to the north and large ponds to the west.

In the 1840s it was the home of an accountant and later the doctor James Partington and continued as a family residence well into the 20th century.

Sadly it has not fared well. Today it looks like any of those old buildings taken into municipal charge and knocked about with scant regard for what it had once been like. Little if anything of the interior is left and the house sits on the edge of Chorlton Park pretty much ignored and forgotten.

Nor have the farm houses which dotted the area lasted the

course. Most vanished in the early 20th century with some like Park Brow on the corner of Sandy Lane and St Werburghs Road undergoing a less than sympathetic conversion into smaller properties.

All of which has distanced The Hall from it rural past and yet for most of its 400 years The Hall was very much part of that agricultural economy.

The Mosleys used their wealth to buy up the manors of Withington, Cheetham and Cheetwood and went on to maximise the income from these lands asserting old rights and increasing fines.[36]

And long after they had vanished from the scene and the land was part of the vast Egerton estate, the tenants of The Hall continued to farm a mix or arable meadowland and orchards.

In the 1840s Henry Jackson worked the fields east up to Red Lion Brook, north into what is now Whalley Range, south along Nell Lane and west into what became Chorlton Park.

And like his neighbours at Dog House Farm and Park Brow

36 Bowd, Stephen, John Dee and Christopher Saxton's Survey of Manchester, (1596), Northern History, XLII:2, September 2005

most of his crops went to the markets of Manchester just four and a bit miles away.

It was a way of life that lasted well into the late 19th century but one that was increasingly threatened by creeping urbanization which was made possible by the provision of mains water, improved sanitation, the supply of gas and finally the arrival of the railway and the Corporation tram.

In 1880 the railway line from Manchester out across south Manchester to Didsbury and beyond was opened and within two decades tram lines were being laid which linked the city centre to the suburbs.

Mrs Williamson in her book on Fallowfield written in 1886 was certain that with arrival of the line running past The Hall and another planned *"we fear the true country aspect of the place is at an end."* [37]

And even before the railway the Egerton estate was beginning the piecemeal sale of land for building. Early in the 20th century the Sandy Lane colony was established close to The Hall and in 1901 the Manchester Evening News commented that across south Manchester there was *"great enterprises a foot and new roads are being monthly added to the local directory."* [38]

37 ibid Williamson, page 48

38 Chorlton-cum-Hardy, from a series of articles History of the Suburbs of Manchester, Manchester Evening News, September 20th 1901, Archive and Local History Library, Q942 733 951 Ch (318)

The pace of new housing was only slackened during the two world wars. In the inter-war period a great swathe of new development occurred to the north of the railway line matched by an expansion of social housing to the south of The Hall, and with all that came new parades of shops cinemas and large new public houses like the Southern Hotel, the Princess and the Mersey Hotel.

Nor was that all for just a little to the east of The Hall came our aerodrome.

The site had been chosen by the War Department in 1917 partly because this was still open farmland and also because of the railway line which meant the aircraft could be transported direct from factories in Newton Heath and Stockport to the airfield and assembled on site.

Its operational life had two short periods. It lasted as a military aerodrome for just a year from May 1918 till May 1919, and operated as civil airfield until 1924.

During the later phase it operated flights to London, Southport, Blackpool and Amsterdam. But for great chunks of this time there was uncertainty about its future. Almost as soon as civilian aircraft began using the aerodrome there was a debate about whether it should be taken over by Manchester Corporation.

Much was made of its closeness to the city centre and the

boost it could give to the economy. Birmingham Council had already bought the West Bromwich Aerodrome and this was a 40 minute car ride from the centre compared to just the ten minutes it would take to get to Albert Square. There was also a strong belief that the Air Ministry would sell for a very low price.

But reading the newspaper reports of the period there is a sense that it was still not as successful as it could be.

One journalist commented that "*the aerodrome has known many vicissitudes. The travellers on the railway between Manchester and Withington have seen it alternate between a place of stirring activity during and just after the war and a place of flat desolation untroubled by the whirr of a single propeller, the great sliding doors of the hangars firmly closed, the weather gauges streaming out in indication of breezes that*

interested no one. Now and then awakened by the measure activity of a civilian service or its pulse has been quickened to a very swift beat by it being a station for the round Britain air Race." [39]

Part of the problem I suspect was just the cost of flying. A flight from Manchester to Paris would shave six to seven hours off the journey by rail and channel crossing but the fare would be 9 guineas making it a third more expensive than the conventional trip. Moreover this assumed that the service had been subsidised *"by £10,000 to cover the installation and inauguration of a service."* Which even then might as one newspaper reported only be used by businessmen *"whose time is worth money, earns say £2000 a year, which is £2 an hour, [who would] save six hours and so make between £8 and £9 on the deal."* [40]

The case became even more important with the development of the surrounding area for housing. Soon the argument ran there would not be enough land for an airport.

39 Alexandra Park Aerodrome, Ministry's Lease Expiring, The Manchester Guardian August 22 1924

40 The Alexandra Park Aerodrome. Pros and Cons of Purchase, The Manchester Guardian September 27th 1922

The Egerton estate appeared to view with favour a Corporation buy up and promised to hold off selling the land till a decision could be made.

But in the event there was no Corporation buy out and by the terms of the original lease agreement all flying use stopped five years after the war's end and on September 24th 1924 all the buildings and power plant were put up for auction including *"nine hangars and other buildings, two generators, cables electric fittings, boilers, heating piping, water piping, baths, wash basins, lavatory fittings and other items."* [41]

The station which had been so important to the aerodrome did not escape change. In July 1923 the name Alexandra Park Railway Station was changed to Wilbraham Road and it closed finally in 1958.

It's one last buzz of activity coming when Granada used it for the venue of its Blues show in 1964.

By then The Hall had but a few years left as a farm house and what had once been a grand house set in open countryside had been reduced to a tired looking property increasingly forgotten and hemmed in by urban sprawl.

41 Sales by Auction, The Manchester Guardian September 6th 1924

PART SEVEN

The Future

A campaign to buy The Hall, some exciting ideas for its future use as a community centre and a look back to its beginnings.

The Hall has stood for over four centuries and has pretty much been all things to all people.

It began as the home of a wealthy entrepreneur who walked with royalty and was rewarded for his service with a knighthood and a bed, became a farmhouse for almost half its existence and has briefly served as a restaurant, night club and even a suite of offices.

Along the way there were those who wanted to turn it into an art gallery and museum, a student hall of residence and even a motel.

And now there is an opportunity to give The Hall a new future.

After the closure of the last restaurant venture in 2011 the building has been empty, lacking a buyer or a purpose.

But a group of local people have come together to save the building by buying it and offering it up for community use.

There is in their words a *"lack of accessible and affordable space for community meetings, exhibitions, rehearsal and*

social events for small, community-orientated enterprises, particularly start-ups." [42]

The Hall would offer just such accommodation and in doing so save what is an important and historic building, becoming a *"community hub, creating a vibrant and welcoming space for a wide range of people to meet, mix, work and play, serving the people of Chorlton and South Manchester."*

Now that is quite an attractive idea not only because it will provide an important use for this empty building but also because it puts The Hall back at the heart of the area.

And as a start and part of a rolling programme the organisers are committed to a series of heritage activities which will promote the history of The Hall and engage local people by calling on their collective memories of the place.

42 Hough End Hall: lets make it ours!
https://spacehive.com/HoughEndHall_lets_make_it_ours#Project promoter

These will build into a permanent exhibition and sit alongside a series of heritage walks through Chorlton and Withington explaining the evolution of The Hall and its place in the story of south Manchester.

This book is a contribution to raising that awareness and the profits from its sale will go to funding the campaign and perhaps to the purchase of The Hall.

In many ways this is the most fortuitous moment for such an exciting project. There is a growing interest in our heritage and already the campaign has encouraged people to share their pictures, memories and stories of their Hough End Hall.

At the same time the arrival of the Metrolink will open up The Hall and the immediate vicinity to a wider audience, some

of whom are drawn here by the small and quirky independent shops along Beech Road and Burton Road, others by the cafes, restaurants and bars of Chorlton and neighbouring Didsbury and many more by the rich cultural events ranging from Chorlton Book Fortnight, Chorlton Arts Festival, the Didsbury Show and the Edge Theatre Company.

A new vibrant community centre in the historic Hough End Hall will play its part in continuing to make this part of south Manchester a vibrant place to live and visit.

And in the fullness of time we might yet see the treasures of the old Hall including Sir Nicholas' 400 year old bed and furniture return to its original home.

Now that would really be historic.

Save
for Chorlton
Community

Let's make it ours! A synopsis by Peter Topping.

Before I talk about the sequence of events I would like to explain who and what we are.

Friends of Hough End Hall is a new, resident led community association, serving the needs of residents of Chorlton and the surrounding areas of south Manchester. Our purpose is to contribute to the quality of life and sustainable regeneration in south Manchester through the use of Hough End Hall as a resource for the community .

At a meeting of Chorlton Civic Society in January 2014 Carolyn turned to me and said "Did you know Peter that Hough End Hall is still up for sale for less than £300,000. Wouldn't it make a fantastic Community Hub?"

And that was the beginning of a roller coaster campaign and for the price of a terrace house off Beech Road we could own a Grade II* listed 16th Century Manor House.

Neither of us having that sort of disposable income to throw at the project and realising that having been left empty for 2 years it would need lots of TLC to bring it back into a habitable state, let alone its former glory, we decided to explore the possibilities with the local community.

In February we met with groups of residents, with local councillors, with our local regeneration officer and with a representative from the Architectural Heritage Fund, a body which helps bring heritage buildings into community use. We shared our ideas at a meeting of Chorlton Civic Society who agreed to back the project. We completed a proposal to the City Council to name Hough End Hall as a community asset of value to the local community for cultural and recreational purposes.

We contacted the selling agents and they said that The Hall was up for sale by RBS and the asking price was £300,000 but indicated that because there was so little interest we could get it for £295,000.

In order to drum up support for our project We decided to form a new association, Friends of Hough End Hall and broadcast our idea on the social media sites. And so in March We built a website – www.houghendhall.org. A Facebook site Hough End Hall revival and a Twitter account @ourheh. Chorlton Community Index and the Chorlton Civic Society newsletter both carried short articles about the campaign. We produced leaflets, posters, badges and a jigsaw.

Our campaign worked so well in raising awareness that it attracted lots of attention even from property buyers that had never heard of The Hall before!

By the time March arrived we had the support of our local MP Mr John Leech and all the local and neighbouring councillors. We had consulted with Locality, Co-operative Shares and MACC (the support body for the community and voluntary sector in Manchester). Michael Thompson offered to help us with strategic planning. Anne Strachan from Crowdfunding UK worked with us to bring Crowdfunding into our plans from various sources.

We were well into our community consultation and ideas were coming in thick and fast for the future of The Hall.

In April we submitted a bid to the Social Investment Business (SIB) for a pre-feasibility grant to pay for surveys of The Hall and support for developing our organisation, policies and business plan. Thanks to Can Do Communities for working with us on this.

We met with Siemens, Southways Housing Trust and Manchester College to discuss how we might work together and collaborate. We continued our community consultation by

holding stalls at the monthly community market outside the Post Box Cafe, and at the Chorlton Big Green Happening. Preserving and re-using old buildings is a central plan of a 'green' Chorlton, and it is great to be a part of a movement for a sustainable future. We gathered in the results of the community consultation and this gave us an indication of the enthusiasm from the local community. There were lots of ideas for various uses and we proceeded to consult on people's preferences for the different uses proposed.

Now was the time to get in touch with the seller, Royal Bank of Scotland, and Carolyn took a trip to London to talk to RBS, to ensure they were in no doubt about our seriousness and the commitment of local people. They seemed to show interest in the possibility of a community use for the Hall.

At the same time, only four months into the campaign, we worked with the Civic Society, and were successful in persuading Manchester City Council to place The Hall on the Register of Assets of Community Value, as a community asset. This meant there was now external recognition for how important The Hall is for the residents of Chorlton and surrounding Districts.

The Council then issued a public notice informing any community interest groups that are legally incorporated, to let them know by the 1st of July if they wished to express interest

to submit a bid for The Hall. After that, the owners could not conclude a sale with anyone other than a community interest group until November 2014.

We formed a not-for-profit limited company, were awarded a grant of £10,000 from SIB which enabled us to undertake preliminary work needed to put a bid in for The Hall, met with the Heritage Lottery Fund and prepared a Crowdfunding campaign.

Taking advantage of the Register of Assets of Community Value, in June, we expressed our interest in buying The Hall to RBS, the current owners and started to use the £10,000 feasibility grant knowing that we had until November to secure funds to buy Hough End Hall.

After great coverage in the local media we were told by the agents "Before you started the campaign we were getting 1 viewing every 3 months and now it has increased to 3 views per week". Perhaps we were in the wrong business!

Rather than helping us to raise funds to buy The Hall we seemed to be raising it's commercial value. Carolyn received several enquiries from potential purchasers asking her to arrange a viewing of The Hall!

June, July and most of August was spent preparing a large bid to the Heritage Lottery Fund to purchase, restore and renovate The Hall. Six months into the project and the Heritage Lottery bid was sent, with support from many groups and

WEDNESDAY, JUNE 11, 2014 THE ADVERTISER

8

Historic hall friends plan social 'hub'

HELEN JOHNSON
helen.johnson@menmedia.co.uk
@helenj13MEN

CAMPAIGNERS are trying to raise hundreds of thousands of pounds to buy a historic hall for community use.

Chorlton residents have launched a major campaign to buy the Grade II listed Hough End Hall and stop it from being sold off privately, after the owners put it on the market.

They hope to raise £400,000 to buy the 428-year-old hall, which is partly hidden behind an office block on Nell Lane in Chorlton.

The Friends of Hough End Hall want to transform it into a thriving hub for community events, functions and social ventures.

Possible ideas include creating an 'Afflecks' style emporium on the upper floor, or allowing musicians to use part of the hall as a rehearsal space.

Chorlton Civic Society managed to get the hall listed on Manchester City Council's register of Assets of Community Value last month.

This means the building's owner, West Register, which is part of the RBS group, cannot conclude a sale with another buyer for six months.

Friends of Hough End Hall group chairman Peter Topping said: "There is so much interest in bringing it back.

"It's got the potential to be something for everyone in the community."

The hall, originally the home of the Mosley family, is one of the oldest in Manchester.

It was last used as a restaurant but has stood empty for several years.

The friends have been awarded £10,000 from Social Investment Business, and are in talks with Heritage Lottery and Crowdfunding UK. Now they are inviting residents, schools and businesses to join their campaign.

For more information or to help, contact Carolyn Kagan on 0161 881 6887, email houghendhall@gmail.com or see the website houghendhall.org.

● Peter Topping and Carolyn Kagan, from the Friends of Hough End Hall, open up the doors at the 428-year-old site

organisations, including Chorlton and Withington Civic Societies, Manchester City Council, Manchester College, Manchester Archives, the Pump House Museum, Manchester Museum of Costume, and some local schools and businesses.

The bad news was that the asset freeze was until November but we weren't likely to here from the Heritage Lottery Fund until early December. We needed more time.

We enlisted the support of Lord Bradley who was first elected to Old Moat Ward in Withington which was part of the estate run from Hough End Hall when Sir Nicholas was Lord of the manor. We also petitioned the Chief Executive of RBS (raising 500 signatures in 10 days) and took our cause to George Osborne, Chancellor of the Exchequer, who has a direct interest in the activities of RBS on behalf of the British public who own most of the bank! The Chancellor wrote to RBS.

We were told by RBS "we had pressed all the right panic buttons in the PR department".

As soon as the Heritage Lottery fund bid was in, we started our Crowdfunding campaign on the Spacehive site. This was to pay for some free standing heritage activities, some further project feasibility work and more specialised surveys of The Hall.

October 2014 and the result of the petition and pressure on RBS was that they agreed to withhold the sale of The Hall to any other buyer until we had heard the outcome of our Heritage Lottery Bid in December.

14   WEDNESDAY, JULY 23, 2014 THE ADVERTISE

Manor house mission

in brief

HELEN JOHNSON
helen.johnson@menmedia.co.uk
@helenjB3M3t

'We are looking at the stories behind the doors'

CAMPAIGNERS seeking to stop a historic hall being sold off privately are piecing together its history.

The Friends of Hough End Hall launched a major campaign to raise more than £300,000 to buy and restore the Grade II listed hall and bring it into community use.

Now historian Andrew Simpson and artist Peter Topping are working together on a series of works which feature the hall in Chorlton and its surroundings.

They are producing a book, a history walk, an exhibition containing photos, paintings, illustrations and architectural drawings, as well as the history and modern day stories of the hall.

The educational tools will aim to help educate people in south Manchester about the history of the 17th century manor house, which was put up for sale earlier this year.

Andrew said: "We are looking at the stories behind the doors.

"Not only into the past history of this vast estate but bringing the story right up to date to include this present moment in time."

Andrew and Peter are looking for people to share their memories and pictures of the hall, and allow them to be published for the community.

The profits from the project will be re-invested into the campaign.

If successful, plans for the hall include creating rehearsal space for musicians, an 'Afflecks' style emporium and venue for community events.

For more information see houghendhall.org, follow @ourheh on Twitter or join the campaign's Facebook group.

TRAFFORD RESIDENTS are being invited to turn off their lights to commemorate the centenary of the First World War.

The council is inviting residents to switch off their lights, apart from a single bulb or candle, between 10pm and 11pm on Monday, August 4, as a mark of respect.

Lancashire Cricket Club, Manchester United, Trafford Town Hall and the Imperial War Museum North are among those taking part.

The lights out event commemorates a famous remark made by then British Foreign Secretary Sir Edward Grey: "The lamps are going out all over Europe.

"We shall not see them lit again in our life-time."

● Painting of Hough End Hall, by Peter Topping, who is working with historian Andrew Simpson to try to save the 17th century manor house

"Any genuine like for like quotes will be beaten"

GUARANTEED

The new year started with some devastating news, unfortunately we did not meet what was a very ambitious target with the Crowdfunding and even worse we were not successful this time in winning a very large Heritage Lottery grant, which was heavily subscribed, for purchase, renovation and initial running costs for The Hall, but perhaps all was not lost.

At the 11th hour a wealthy local businessman who financed a charitable foundation put in a bid for The Hall by the deadline set by RBS, and assured us a place for our community use in his plans. But in the end due to other commercial considerations it was not possible for him to include the purchase of The Hall in his scheme.

We are still committed to work with whoever buys Hough End Hall, and we will still seek to protect, promote and restore the building as an historic community asset.

PART NINE
Paintings, illustrations and pictures of the past

Archive material that didn't fit in the story but was too precious to leave out.

Now with a building which long ago celebrated its 400th birthday The Hall has had plenty of people who have recorded its appearance.

They range from the professional and commercial photographers to those with humble cameras whose "snaps" of the building have sat hidden away for decades.

Added to this have been more than a few artists who with a mix of oils, watercolours or pen and ink have done their bit to capture the magic of this historic place.

And it seemed a shame not to let these come out of the shadows and be seen in what is the first full length book on the history of The Hall.

So here are fifteen which deserve to have their place in the story of Hough End Hall.

Watercolour and ink drawing by J J Alley 1869.

Dated as 1890 probably one of the oldest photographs of The Hall.

Colourized postcard from 1910.

Watercolour by Victor Strange 1913.

Postcard from 1920.

Painting by Evacustes A Phipson 1924.

Hough End Hall, A Fine Old Manchester Manor Hous

FEDERICK E NEILL. 1932..

STRANGE that Hough End Hall, Withington, Manchester, built by Sir Nicholas Mosley in 1596, and the home of Sir Oswald Mosley's ancestors, of the Manor of Manchester for many generations, should have endured its greatest vicissitudes in recent years. In 1921 it was discovered proposed new highway would, if it followed plans, run right through the Hall. A Joint Preservation Board was formed, and as a result of its the new road was diverted to pass a considerable distance in front of the Hall. Manchester owes a debt to this gesture, which preserves for the

Newspaper article with illustration by Frederick E Neil 1932.

Painting by Byron Dawson 1940.

Photograph from T Bradley 1952.

Painting by J Montgomery 1965 from a 1942 Photograph.

Painting by J Montgomery 1965 copied from an old print..

Photo of The Hall 1980.

Photo of The Hall 1990 after refurbishment by CRC North.

Photograph by Peter Topping 2013.

Painting by Peter Topping 2013.

Bibliography

Alexandra Park Aerodrome, Ministry's Lease Expiring, The Manchester Guardian August 22 1924.

Ancient Monuments Society's Transactions, Ancient Monuments' Society, 1975.

Bailey Oliver, private correspondence.

Booker, Rev John, A history of the ancient Chapels of Didsbury and Chorlton, 1857, Chetham Society.

Bowd, Stephen, John Dee and Christopher Saxton's Survey of Manchester, (1596), Northern History, XLII: 2, September 2005.

Bulmer-Thomas, Ivor, letter to the Manchester Evening News, January 1969

Chorlton-cum-Hardy, from a series of articles History of the Suburbs of Manchester, Manchester Evening News, September 20th 1901.

Egerton Papers M24, Archives and Local History Library, Central Reference Library Manchester Libraries.

Hough End: A scheme for saving The Hall, Manchester Guardian March 24, 1921.

Hough End Hall: Let's make it ours! https://spacehive.com/HoughEndHall_lets_make_it_ours#Project promoter

Farrer William & Brownbill ed, A History of the County of Lancaster: Volume 41911.

Manchester Evening News February 1915.

Manchester Guardian, January 20 1849.

Mosley, Sir Oswald, Family Memoirs, 1849, Printed for Private Circulation.

Preservation of Hough End Hall, Manchester Guardian December 19, 1936.

Renshaw, Cliff, FRICS, Hough End Hall 400 Years of History, 2001

Sales by Auction, the Manchester Guardian September 6th 1924.

Simpson, Andrew, The Story of Chorlton-cum-Hardy, the History Press 2012.

Thompson Paul, from a conversation with Andrew Simpson, August 2014.

Tudor Manor Saved Appeal Upheld, Guardian September 29, 1962.

The Alexandra Park Aerodrome. Pros and Cons of Purchase, The Manchester Guardian September 27th 1922.

Waterhouse, Robert, Hall, or nothing at all, the Guardian April 21 1973.

Williamson, Mrs C, Sketches of Fallowfield, John Heywood, 1888,

Index

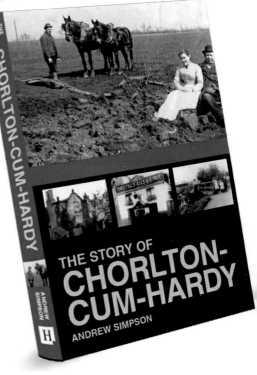